9780550309266

Consultant on this book—
Dr. Paul Witty, Director
Psycho-Educational Clinic
Northwestern University

The "I Want to Be" books are designed to encourage independent reading on beginner level. The concepts—broad as a child's imagination—bring pleasure to early reading experience and better understanding of the world. But the text is in line with the young reader's new skill.

All but eleven of the one-hundred-one words of the vocabulary used in this book are from *The First Thousand Words for Children's Reading.*

I want to be a COAL MINER

By CARLA GREENE

Illustrations by Audrey Williamson

CHILDRENS PRESS, CHICAGO

K184

EMORY UNITED METHODIST CHURCH

Cars of coal
go by.
Cars and cars
and cars.
"Where does
it all go?"
asks Jack.

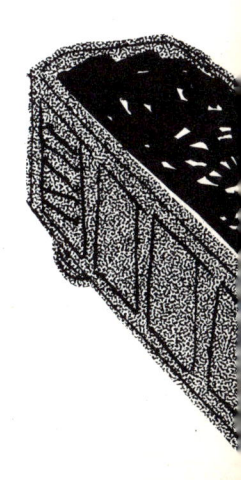

"Coal is used
for many things,"
his father answers.
He draws some
pictures for Jack.
He says, "Coal
gives us heat
and light
and power."

He says, "We get many things from coal."

"But where do we get all this coal?" asks Jack.

"It is in the earth," answers his father.

"Dead plants become coal. They stay under mud and sand for millions of years. They get hard as rock."

Some coal is
easy to reach.
Some coal is
near the top
of the ground.

Some coal

is in a hill.

Some coal is deep down in the earth.

Men go down, down into the earth to get this coal.

Plans are made before the miners go to work.

This is the way

the miners cut

into a wall

of coal.

This is one way
they break up
a wall of coal.
They use an air-gun.

This is the way
the pieces of coal
are picked up.
Then they are taken
to a little train.

The little train

takes the coal out

of the mine.

The coal goes up,
up in a building.
This building is
called a TIPPLE.
Here the rocks are
taken out of the coal,
and it is washed.
Coal of different sizes
goes into railroad cars.
Cars and cars of coal.

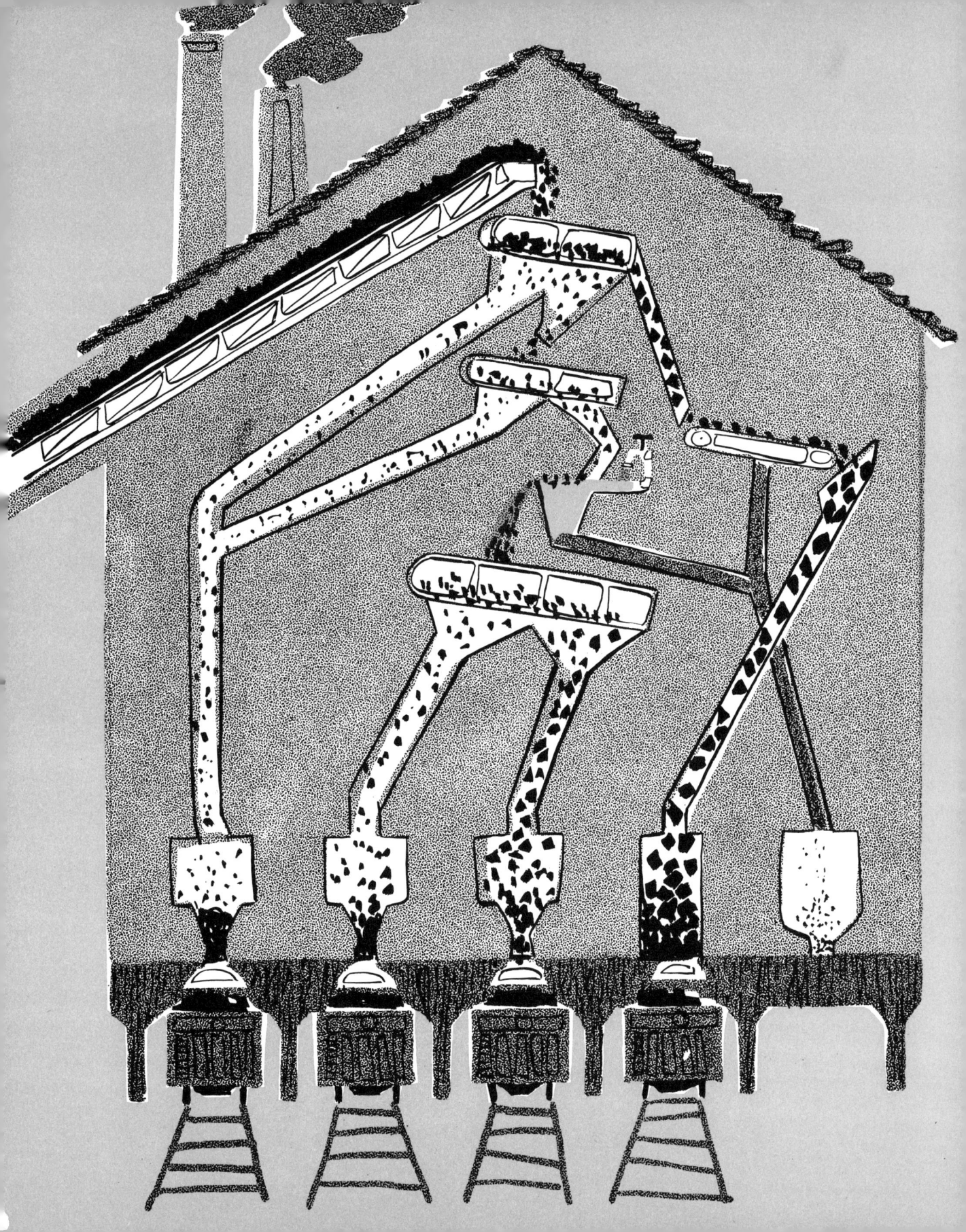

Coal is sent

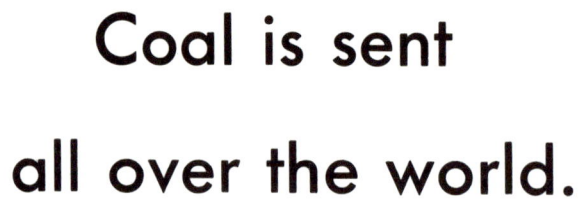

all over the world.

"We cannot get along without coal," says Jack's father.

"Or the coal miners," says Jack. "I want to be a coal miner when I grow up."